BRITAIN IN OLD PHOTOGRAPHS

NORTH GLOUCESTERSHIRE

AT WAR

P E T E R   G I L L

ALAN SUTTON PUBLISHING LIMITED

Alan Sutton Publishing Limited
Phoenix Mill · Far Thrupp · Stroud
Gloucestershire · GL5 2BU

First published 1995

Copyright © Peter Gill, 1995

British Library Cataloguing in Publication Data.
A catalogue record for this book is available from
the British Library.

ISBN 0-7509-1134-4

Typeset in 9/10 Sabon.
Typesetting and origination by
Alan Sutton Publishing Limited.
Printed in Great Britain by
Hartnolls, Bodmin, Cornwall.

The Lord Mayor and the Lady Mayoress
request the pleasure of the Company of

The Worshipful
The Mayor & Mayoress of Cheltenham

at the Mansion House
on Monday, July 20th, at 3 p.m.
in connection with the
Empire Air Raid Distress Fund

R.S.V.P.,
The Lord Luke,
Chairman, Empire Air Raid Distress Fund Flag Day,
36, Kingsway, W.C.2.

Tea

Contents

Cheltenham. After the bombing raid on the town on the night of 11 December 1940, this unexploded bomb was found and recovered in The Reddings, North Road. Standing with the bomb is Gladys Townsend. Her father, Mr Sevordy, is standing to the right of her. The other lady in the picture is Mrs Webb.

Introduction

Almighty God, bless and guard my loved ones at home. Give me grace and strength to do my duty in what I believe to be a righteous cause; make me strong of heart and fearless in danger; and whether I live or die keep me in Thine almighty keeping, through Jesus Christ Our Lord. Amen.
– A wartime prayer from the Chaplain of the Fleet, September 1939

The first problem encountered in putting together this two-volume photographic collection of Gloucestershire during the Second World War was finding a cut-off point between north and south Gloucestershire. I chose Cheltenham as being the most southern town of north Gloucestershire, and drew a reasonably straight line through the map at the base of Cheltenham's conurbation. This was no great academic decision, but a convenient dividing line to separate the photographic subjects of this large county into two books. Places you do not find in this book will be found in *South Gloucestershire at War*.

The second problem was collecting a number of photographs that gave a fair portrayal of life throughout the north Gloucestershire area during the war. Unfortunately, in any project like this it is impossible to get a photographic record of all events happening in all areas, but when wartime film rationing, financial shortages and restrictions as to what could and what could not be photographed are added, then the task became even more difficult to complete. Comparatively few photographs were taken in wartime Britain, but of those that survived, I have used about 200 in compiling this book.

My aim was to give as good a picture of life in north Gloucestershire during the war as possible. I would have liked to have included photographs of installations such as anti-aircraft guns, searchlights, pill boxes, airfields and the 'mountains' of rocks built in fields throughout the county to stop enemy gliders from landing, as well as more photographs of prisoners of war and allied servicemen who were living in the county. Unfortunately my quest for these was not fruitful, but I am still very much interested in seeing such photographs if they actually exist.

The first section of the collection concerns the children of the war, both those who came to Gloucestershire as evacuees from Bristol, Birmingham and London, and those who had always lived in the county. For the evacuees it was a time of great upheaval and uncertainty; they were given to strangers to be looked after in homes often very different from the ones they were used to. In some cases the evacuees didn't see their parents again until the end of the war. For the children already living in the county it was often a time of excitement with many 'morale-lifting' parties and fund-raising efforts. They were still too young to realize the implications and worries of war.

Section Two portrays everyday life, showing some of the transport in use, the workers, some of the many weddings that took place. I have tried to give a feel of the type of people that lived in the county and how they worked, rested and played.

The Dig for Victory campaign is the subject of Section Three: the importance the campaign was given in schools and the nationwide urge for any possible scrap of land to be used for raising crops and produce. Many Land Army girls were drafted into the county to help local farmers – I have tried to depict the *esprit de corps* they developed and the hard nature of the work they had to do. For this purpose I have included a small number of photographs of girls stationed in Upton-on-Severn who were given regular work details in Gloucestershire along with photographs of girls living and working in the county.

Section Four gives a hint of the wide variety of sport that was encouraged in the county. Sport of all kinds was deemed important both in keeping the population fit and in keeping morale high by giving people something to concentrate on instead of their hardships.

The home services of Section Five are the men and women who voluntarily gave up their time to serve the country on the home front. Some joined the ARP, some the Home Guard; others became volunteer firefighters, first aiders, special constables, and some entered the Women's Volunteer Services – the contributions of all were invaluable. Also included in this section are the regular police and fire services that kept the county safe and secure.

Section Six illustrates in a small way the massive commitment given by Gloucestershire's servicemen who were willing to give up their lives for the security of Britain, many rushing to get married before rushing off to war.

Section Seven shows some scenes of wartime north Gloucestershire, and the last section deals with some of the special events – of a happier nature – that happened during the war.

These photographs are only a taste of the period 1939–45 and by no means the complete story; it would have been nice to have been able to focus more on other events in other villages, but should I be fortunate to come across these photographs then this could be a future project.

Peter Gill, August 1995

CHILDREN OF THE WAR

Winchcombe. A young evacuee, six-month-old Jean Armstrong, the daughter of Sgt. Armstrong RASC, and Mrs Armstrong of London. Jean was evacuated along with her mother to the Postlip Hall Maternity Home in order to be brought into this world. Mother and baby were then accommodated at The Martens, in Winchcombe, the home of Miss Eleanor Adlard.

Puckrup. These young Bristolians were evacuated in 1941 to Puckrup Hall, the home of the Revd P. Wigan and his wife. The hall catered for many young evacuees under the guidance of the matron Miss M.K. Sampson of Cheltenham, who is seen holding one of the babies.

Puckrup. More of the Bristol babies evacuated to Puckrup Hall. To help her with her charges the matron had two staff nurses, three probationers and several voluntary nurses at her disposal.

Cheltenham. In February 1941 the American Women's Hospital Fund sent new shoes and warm clothing to Cheltenham to be distributed to evacuated children in the town. The distribution was superintended by Dr Mary Christie, seen on the right wearing the armband, at The Elms in Cheltenham. Mrs D.L. Lipson of the Women's Volunteer Service is helping the children in the centre of the picture.

Gotherington. Dennis (left) and Ron Baird in the back porch of Mrs Hayman's Cotswold Cottage. The brothers were evacuated from Dagenham to Gotherington on 15 June 1940 and stayed with Mrs Hayman, where life was disciplined and regimental, for approximately two years. Dennis and Ron were among five of the seven boys in the Baird family that were evacuated to Gloucestershire; Joe, one of the brothers, returned to Gotherington in 1993 to marry a lady he had known as a 12-year-old, after renewing her acquaintance during a fiftieth-anniversary trip to Gotherington in 1990.

Cheltenham. Evacuated Birmingham boys outside the hall in Milsom Street where they were temporarily schooled in the autumn of 1939. The hall is now used as a community centre. Gordon Baker, sitting sixth from the right in the front row, was evacuated to Cheltenham along with his sister from Aston, Birmingham on 1 September 1939. Gordon was housed with the East family in Elmfield Road, but only stayed with them until June 1940 when he was sent to a boys' camp in Rugeley, Cannock.

Cheltenham. A garden party for evacuated and local children at St Matthew's Church in 1941 or 1942. The girl at the far right of the picture is Dorothy Baker, the younger sister of Gordon on the previous page. She stayed in Cheltenham for the whole duration of the war – about 5½ years, for the most part living with a family in Devonshire Street.

Cheltenham. On Monday 30 December 1940, 600 evacuees and children of servicemen were entertained at the Cheltenham Town Hall. This picture shows some of them being given sweets and oranges after the show.

Tewkesbury. In January 1941 the Revd R.W. Taylor, in the centre of this picture, organized some entertainment for the senior child evacuees that were being schooled at Tewkesbury's elementary school. This picture of Mr Taylor and the evacuees was taken in the Abbey schoolroom.

Prestbury. A New Year's party for evacuees in January 1941. The party took place in the Prestbury Women's Institute Hall and was paid for by the Evacuees Entertainment Fund and the WI.

Cheltenham. Testing and adjusting children's gas masks in February 1941 at the St John's Institute. Alec Wilson, the senior warden of the All Saints South District is standing, far left.

Sevenhampton. A school photograph of Sevenhampton School pupils and their teachers, April 1941. The headmistress, Mrs Cathcart, is in the centre; to the left is fellow teacher Mrs Grainger.

Cheltenham. Pupils of St Gregory's School enjoying a communal dinner in February 1941. From Christmas 1940 the school provided a daily lunchtime meal for more than one hundred of its pupils who either lived some distance from the school or whose mothers were at work. Lunch was generally a hot meal consisting of two courses.

Chipping Campden. Jean and her brother Joe Tucker sitting on the war memorial in Chipping Campden shortly after an Armistice Sunday during the war. Their father was the village postmaster and so they lived in a fairly large house that doubled as the sorting office.

Chipping Campden. Jean Tucker and some friends playing at the back of her house in 1943. The name of the house has since been changed to London House. The girl in the centre facing the camera is Tess Collett, a neighbour of the Tuckers, whose father was the village baker. Holding her left hand is Margaret Smith, the daughter of one of the village policemen. At this time the Campden police station was staffed by four policemen, and it had the dubious privilege of having the village air raid siren attached to its front. Jean Tucker is holding Tess Collett's right hand.

Chipping Campden. Young girls maypole dancing in the main square of Chipping Campden. The square is now used as off-road parking. In many ways the villagers of Chipping Campden weren't affected greatly by the war. There were obvious limitations with food and fuel rationing, but the villagers comprised a largely self-sufficient country community. Jean Tucker remembers her mother often exchanging a cake for a pint of milk with a local farmer's wife.

Tewkesbury. In April 1941 Tewkesbury staged a War Weapons Week, dedicated to raising morale and showing off armaments and tools of war as well as raising money for the war effort. These children are interested in the wreckage of a German Messerschmitt aircraft.

Tewkesbury. A tea party held for the children of Tewkesbury during the war. The event was organized and sponsored by the Royal British Legion. Standing at the back right is Fred Green, a notable member of the Tewkesbury branch of the British Legion and known and admired in the town for his many charitable efforts.

Kemerton. A New Year's party in January 1941 for the children of Kemerton. Fifty children over the age of seven were entertained at the Victoria Hall by managers of the village's Church of England school. There was a fancy dress parade and prizes were given for the best costumes.

Kemerton. In March 1941 the schoolchildren of Kemerton put on a small concert at the Victoria Hall in order to raise money for Tewkesbury hospital. The concert was produced and directed by Mrs V.A. Long and her husband Phillip H. Long played the piano. These children are members of the cast of a short play entitled 'The Golden Goose'.

Tewkesbury. Participants of the children's fancy dress parade, organized to commemorate Tewkesbury's War Weapons Week in April 1941. The little boy second from the left heralds the gratitude felt for the USA – Britain still stood alone against Nazi Germany, but we were much dependent on the Lend-Lease programme and charitable efforts by American citizens.

Tewkesbury. Three of the prize winners in the War Weapons Week fancy dress parade. The parade itself was held at Tewkesbury Town Hall. Note that the tone of the costumes is very morale-boosting and full of spirit. The aim of the week was to raise £40,000 towards defeating Hitler.

Tewkesbury. More participants for the fancy dress parade. The War Weapons Week was held from 29 March until 5 April 1941.

Tewkesbury. Girls participating in the fancy dress parade. Bearing in mind rationing and the shortage of clothing, the ingenuity and skill in making these costumes is quite remarkable. Often, everyday clothes would be home-made from material off-cuts, black-out material and very occasionally, if lucky, parachute silk.

Kemerton. In December 1941 these pupils of the Grange School in Kemerton produced a Christmas show entitled 'Where the Rainbow Ends'. The show was put on in the village hall and raised money for the Red Cross Association.

Chipping Campden. A wartime picture of the Chipping Campden Boy Scouts. Standing second from the right is Joe Tucker and the blond boy at the back is his brother George. George was later enlisted and sent to India from where he would often send his mother packages of beautiful material which she made into dresses.

Winchcombe. In September 1941 the First Winchcombe Wolf Cubs made a concerted effort to help salvage paper. The Cubs were led by their Cub master Mrs R.S. Pullom who is seen here helping to load a truck.

Winchcombe. More members of Winchcombe Cub Scouts helping in the drive to save and re-use waste paper. Later during the war a salvage van would come round the town collecting waste paper and cardboard.

Tewkesbury. A group photograph of the Tewkesbury and District Girl Guides, taken on the occasion of the visit of the Princess Royal to Tewkesbury Abbey on 12 May 1941.

Tewkesbury. On the same occasion this group photograph of the Tewkesbury Brownies was taken. The Brownies and Guides welcomed the Princess to the abbey and later met and were inspected by her.

WARTIME LIFE

Leigh. Farmer's daughter Muriel Brunt of Evington Hill Farm, Leigh, with a quantity of waste metal that she collected to help with the national salvage effort. Everyone was encouraged to save and salvage as much as possible whether it was metal, paper, cardboard, wood or potato peelings that could be fed to pigs.

Cheltenham. In July 1941 four tons of steel arrived in Cheltenham in the form of 5,000 helmets. These were to be supplied to the town's voluntary fire-watchers and were stored temporarily at the fire brigade headquarters.

Winchcombe. These three women, evacuees from Eastbourne, were the first women in Gloucestershire north of Cheltenham to be employed as road workers. They commenced work on the roads of Winchcombe in October 1941 doing the lighter work. They are, from left to right, Mrs Barnard, Mrs Walz and Miss Duke; with them is the foreman Mr F. Humphries.

Cheltenham. Self-sufficiency was the real catchword during the war and everyone was greatly encouraged to produce food from any possible quarter. This herd of goats belonged to A.M.R. Rotheram of Gloucester Road. They were of a Swiss breed renowned for their capacity for producing milk.

Cheltenham. A row of four Black and White coaches with masked headlamps in accordance with black-out instructions. New in 1937, they operated for the early part of the war; however, as hostilities intensified, the coach services were withdrawn and a number of the coaches were converted for use as ambulances. (Photograph courtesy of the C.F. Martin Collection.)

Winchcombe. This Bedford coach was bought by Alf Gillett of Winchcombe in 1938 and was used throughout the war to ferry people between Winchcombe and Cheltenham for a fee of 9d single and 1s 6d return. Alf Gillett himself would drive his coaches and he was hugely liked and respected. On his last trip back from Cheltenham at night he would always ensure that he never left anyone behind, and he was often stopped by the police at the top of Cleeve Hill with an overladen coach. Some of his passengers would be told to get off, but then Alf would always come back to pick them up once he had emptied his coach in Winchcombe. (Photograph courtesy of the C.F. Martin Collection.)

Stow-on-the-Wold. Victor Fluck of Notgrove standing between two of the coaches that he and his mother operated as 'Fluck's of Stow' during the war. Both vehicles have masked headlamps. On the left is a Leyland coach that seated 31, which was bought by Fluck's second-hand in 1938; on the right is a Bedford 26-seater which was bought new in early 1939. (Photograph courtesy of the C.F. Martin Collection.)

Tewkesbury. Ernie Hartell standing with a 1936 Leyland coach that he drove throughout the war for Warner's of Tewkesbury. The coach had been bought new in 1936 and continued to operate until 1954. (Photograph courtesy of C.F. Martin Collection.)

Winchcombe. The Barnes family of 53 Hailes Street in 1944, from left to right: Arthur, Noel (Alan), Brenda, Barbara, Evelyn and Ethel. The family moved from West Bromwich to Winchcombe when the bombing became so bad that it made Brenda very ill. Arthur was given the job of manager of Winchcombe's only cinema at The Old Tanneries in Silk Mill Lane. He was often helped by one of the German prisoners of war barracked on the Sudeley Castle grounds, Hans Hanagarth. Behind the cinema, the American troops stationed in the town had their cookhouse and canteen.

Winchcombe. Two wartime workers outside the Old Flour Mill in Winchcombe, Gwen Yeend on the left and Evelyn Barnes on the right. Both women started work at the mill in early 1945. Work conditions were not great in the mill: during the winter, the only heating came from a small stove, and after a day's work they would always be plastered head to foot in flour.

Winchcombe. Evelyn and Gwen again outside the Old Mill. After work, the girls would often rush home to get washed and changed in order to go down to the Winchcombe Dance Hall where the Winchcombe 'Goodfellows Band' would often be playing. The band consisted of Harry Bridges on drums, Alf Gobbins on piano and Burt Goodfellow on the piano accordion. The dance hall had a special sprung floor and was a favourite venue until it was later turned into a packing store for the flour mill.

Cheltenham. The office staff of the Black and White Coach Company of Cheltenham, August 1944. First on the left is Marion Smith (later Lewis) who worked as a secretary and accountant for the company.

Cheltenham. A Dowty's staff photograph at Arle Court in wartime. George Dowty is sitting in the front row, fifth from the left.

Cheltenham. The hydraulic assembly and testing shop at Dowty's Arle Court in March 1940.

Cheltenham. Women workers being trained at Dowty's in March 1941. At the height of their employment, women accounted for 50 per cent of all workers at Dowty's.

Cheltenham. Scenes from one of Dowty's engineering shops. Note the high ratio of women to men workers. During the war, most women were required to take on full-time jobs to help offset the loss of male employees to the armed services. Wives and mothers now filled up spaces in assembly lines as well as having to bring up families, feed husbands and see to household chores.

Winchcombe. A photograph of Evelyn Barnes from Winchcombe illustrating her two left feet! During the war in Cheltenham High Street there was a favourite shoe shop of the young Miss Barnes, which was nicknamed the 'muddle shoe shop'. In the front window of this shop would be thrown a quantity of shoes available to the purchaser at half-coupon rate. The problem was you had to search through the mound of shoes to find a matching pair in design and size. On one occasion Evelyn bought such a pair of shoes only to get home and find that both shoes fitted the left foot. This was before the time when you could return and exchange goods and she certainly didn't have the money to buy a different pair – so she had to wear two left feet!

Cheltenham. Members of the St Catherine's Home Committee of Cambray, at the Municipal Offices on the occasion of their annual general meeting in November 1941. Left to right are Sister A. Bannister, Miss E.M. Rowbotham, Revd J.S. Fowler, Miss J. Estcourt, Canon J.B. Goodliffe, Revd S.J. Richards and Sister G. Jefferies.

Prestbury. Seven members of the Prestbury Women's Institute who produced a theatrical show consisting of three sketches, performed on Monday 10 March 1941. The thespians from left to right are Mrs Bissett, Miss Betty Gibbons, Mrs G. Readings, Mrs Proust, Miss E. Garner, Miss Wilton and Miss I. Sawyer.

Winchcombe. One of the many weddings that took place during the war, this one of the Barnes family, latterly of Winchcombe. Second from left is Dais Barnes and to her right are her sisters Evelyn and Barbara (Evelyn is holding Barbara). The next bridesmaid is Brenda who is standing next to her mother Ethel. The little boy being held above Ethel is her son Alan. The wedded couple are Ray and Ida Barnes.

Tewkesbury. Married at the Abbey in July 1941 were A.M. Nind of Tewkesbury and Doris Baldrey of Gloucester. This photograph was taken at their reception at The Bell Hotel in Tewkesbury.

Bourton-on-the-Water.
Mr Goronwy Owen Jones and
his new wife Mabel after their
wedding at St Lawrence's
Church in Bourton-on-the-
Water in June 1941. The
photographer was the Bourton-
based W.J. Butt.

Cheltenham. 'Frankie's Wedding' of 6 April 1940 is how Marion Smith (later Lewis)
recorded and remembered this photograph. Marion was the maid of honour (third from
the right) to her best friend Frankie.

Cheltenham. At the height of the European hostilities on 30 March 1941, Mr and Mrs James Cox of 3 Fairfield Parade in Cheltenham celebrated their golden wedding anniversary. Proud of this achievement, they had this photograph published in the *Cheltenham Chronicle*.

Cheltenham. Another golden wedding anniversary, this time of Mr and Mrs W.H. Bell of Tivoli Street who were married in May 1891 at St Luke's Church. Their two sons and one daughter are pictured with their respective families in this snap. Joe Bell, the eldest son, was the secretary of the Exmouth Arms Bowling Club and a former secretary of Cheltenham Rugby Football Club.

Tewkesbury. A group of Italian prisoners of war engaged in cleaning out a ditch and helping in land reclamation. Italian prisoners were regularly sent out on work details, often in land reclamation or farm labouring. The Italians were camped at Ashchurch (in the huts that still stand today opposite the entrance to Ashchurch Camp) and there was also a POW camp for them in the area that is now the play area in the grounds of the Canterbury Leys pub.

Winchcombe. Some of the many German prisoners of war who were camped on the grounds of Sudeley Castle. As the Allies began to win the war and the number of prisoners swelled, security became reasonably relaxed. The POWs were allowed to wander around Winchcombe and made many friends in the town, some even meeting their future wives. They weren't allowed to buy anything from the shops, however; nor could they wander further than the Feudry Limit signs which were on the town's outskirts.

Moreton-in-Marsh. An Easter bombing campaign in 1941 brought damage to this farm, probably in Moreton-in-Marsh. There were no civilian casualties, only a few unlucky livestock.

Moreton-in-Marsh. The same Easter bombing raid, which was probably no more than aircraft shedding their load before returning home. The field probably belonged to the Mickleton and Oldborough Farm.

Cheltenham. The ruins of the Black and White coach station in St Margaret's Road, which was struck during Cheltenham's worst raid of the war on the night of 11 December 1941. The Bristol No. 79 bus was hurled over a wall by the force of the blast.

DIG FOR VICTORY

Tewkesbury. Under the guidance of Headmaster A.E. Leatham, boys of Tewkesbury Senior County School start work on converting the school's playing field into a cultivable piece of land.

Tewkesbury. The school's field was first dug up in May 1941 as part of the nationwide campaign to put every possible scrap of land to use in growing and producing vital foodstuffs.

Tewkesbury. Mr Leatham was an enthusiastic and knowledgeable gardener and put every effort into producing as much as possible from the school's land. Schools throughout the county had similar projects in hand and most private gardens were put to arable usage.

Tewkesbury. Boys and the headmaster of Tewkesbury Senior County School inspecting one of the school's active beehives. Honey from the bees, as well as other foodstuffs produced at the school, was available to buy in the school shop by parents of pupils.

Tewkesbury. Girls of the Tewkesbury Senior County School displaying some rhubarb that they had grown and were now selling in the school shop. The proceeds from the sale of produce were fed back into the Dig for Victory project to try and achieve an optimum production from the school's land.

Cheltenham. Dean Close School boys on a work detail in 1940 at a farm in Elmstone Hardwicke. The school earned a great reputation helping local farmers harvest crops.

Chipping Campden. A party in the town hall of Chipping Campden put on for the Land Army women billeted in the village and who were working the local farms.

Chipping Campden. The life of landgirls was far from easy – they worked a ten-hour day six days a week; even when parties like this were put on for them, they would have to be back in their communal hostels by 10 p.m.

Upton-on-Severn. Although these Land Army members were barracked at the Old Hall, in Upton, Worcestershire, their work details often brought them the few miles into Gloucestershire to help at farms in the Tewkesbury area.

Tewkesbury. Women in the Land Army enjoying a refreshing break in the hot summer sun. In the back row, left to right, are Lilian Barrett, Rose Ellis and Dusty Rhodes. In the front row are Audrey Cresswell, Vera Francis and an unnamed friend.

River Severn. Somewhere along the banks of a River Severn swollen by floodwater are five Land Army members: Gladys Jones, Dolly Hanks, -?-, Frieda Kendrick and Vera Francis.

River Severn. Vera Francis decked out in her Land Army uniform. Vera volunteered to join the Land Army and was brought from her home in Birmingham to Upton-on-Severn, from where she ventured into Gloucestershire on work details. The fields in Twyning, Shuthonger, Tirley and Corse Lawn all benefited from her labour.

Upton-on-Severn. Anna Tuckey in the driving seat and Vera Francis with one of the lorries that they were required to drive during their service. Vera joined the Land Army in 1942 and stayed in the service until 1950.

Upton-on-Severn. Landgirls Anna Tuckey and Vera Francis, Worcestershire-based, who ventured into Gloucestershire. Many former Land Army women remember the friendships forged during years of service with great affection.

Bishop's Cleeve. Pat Botherway (later Hitchman) in her Land Army uniform in 1941. During her service she lived in digs in Bishop's Cleeve and at The Folly in Gotherington with Mrs Gilbey.

Tewkesbury. Pat Botherway driving a TD14 caterpillar-track tractor down the Tewkesbury Road after having picked it up from Tewkesbury railway station. This tractor was particularly big and difficult to manoeuvre.

Bishop's Cleeve. Pat Botherway on the left and her friend Olive, another landgirl, with one of the Italian prisoners of war that were sent to work along with the women in the fields. Miss Botherway worked many fields around the Cleeve area and on one occasion had to plough up land between US Nissen huts on the site that is now the Benhall GCHQ in Cheltenham.

Bishop's Cleeve. Pat Botherway on the tractor on the left during a display of tractor driving. Both tractors are Fergusons, but the one on the left is fitted with off-road spiked wheels for gripping in muddy conditions, while the one on the left had pneumatic tyres and is registered for use on the highway. They were provided by B.S. Bird who supplied most agricultural tractors in central Gloucestershire.

Woodmancote. Pat Botherway felling and clearing trees on a Caterpillar tractor. The GWAEC lettering on the side of the tractor refers to the Gloucestershire War Agricultural Executive Committee, which controlled and organized agricultural land use in the county. There were two main tractor depots in this particular region, one at Gotherington Fields, the other at Stoke Orchard.

Tewkesbury. Mrs W.S. Morrison, wife of Tewkesbury's postmaster-general, talking to members of the Women's Land Army during the town's War Weapons Week in April 1941.

Cheltenham. R.W. Birt of Prestbury ploughing up a field at Whaddon, adjacent to the Cheltenham Town Football Club ground, so that it could be used as allotments. This work was done under the auspices of the Cheltenham Corporation.

Section Four

SPORT

Cleeve Hill. In June 1941 at the Cotswold Hills Golf Course, a professional four-ball foursome tournament was held in order to raise money for the Red Cross and its War Relief Fund. Here famous professional Henry Cotton is putting at the seventh hole.

Cleeve Hill. The Cotswold Hills golf professional A.F. Parker putting at the eighth hole. The match was played by Alfred Pagham and Henry Cotton against W.J. Cox and A.F. Parker.

Cleeve Hill. A.F. Parker putting at the seventeenth hole. The match ended all square and over £400 was realized for the War Relief Fund.

Bishop's Cleeve. Marion Smith (later Lewis) and a friend enjoying a horse-riding afternoon in Bishop's Cleeve in 1939.

Prestbury. A polo match being played at Prestbury Park, 1939.

Cheltenham. Members of the VP Airscrews cricket team in August 1941. Standing, left to right: E. Grimster, E. Dean, W. Simmons, J. Pritchard, E. Townsend, G. Pardoe, G. Parker. Front row: A.L. Challis, L.T. Aldridge (captain), W. Bishop (honorary secretary).

Cheltenham. A British Empire XI that played a Cheltenham Town cricket team on 14 June 1941. Standing, left to right: D. Jenkins (umpire), P. Millman, N.L. Hills, C.T. Hitchman, H.P. Crabtree, F. Robson. Seated: A.E. Nutter, Capt. W.M.E. White, D.L. Donnelly (captain), T.H. Thipthorpe, E.J. Stephens.

Cheltenham. The Cheltenham Town XI. Standing, left to right: J.O. Hitchcock, C. Hollinshead, F.J. Sewell, A.G.S. Wilcox, P.W. Woof, A.J. Parr (umpire). Seated: W.T. Mustoe, R.E. Yeend, G.B. Bence, C.J. Price (captain), J.W. Smith, W.C. Woof.

Cheltenham. The St Mary's Hall training college hockey team that played Cheltenham and County Harriers' team on 8 November 1941. Left to right: B. Hawes, M. Brooks, A. Ballands, M. Callister, M. Parry, W. Barton, D. Hoare (captain), M. Rufus, D. Gerrard, J.K. Davies, D. Wainwright, M. Ogden (umpire).

Cheltenham. In September 1941 the East Gloucestershire Tennis Club organized a junior tennis tournament. Here, a few of the competitors and spectators pose for the camera.

Cheltenham. Some of the junior tennis competitors; from the left: Ann Lewis and R. Stuart-Taylor (who played together to come second in the mixed doubles), and Ann Mackenzie and D. Vetch.

Cheltenham. Junior girls' competitor Barbara Harper illustrating her renowned serving.

Cheltenham. The officials at the East Gloucestershire Junior Tennis Tournament: Miss Badham, Mrs Douglas Grundy (tournament organizer) and Colonel L.W. Miller.

Cheltenham. Some of the competitors, winners and losers of the 1941 junior tennis tournament at the East Gloucestershire Tennis Club.

Bourton-on-the-Water. The Bourton Rovers football team that played an RAF XI on the village football ground in May 1941.

Bourton-on-the-Water. The RAF XI that played Bourton Rovers. The game was played to raise money for the Red Cross Agricultural Fund.

Woodmancote. The village football team played Whaddon Juniors on Saturday 22 November on the Whaddon recreation ground. Standing, left to right: J. Holder (reserve), E. Trinder, L. Tibbett, G. Sharp, G. Holder, K. Stewart, D. Green, G. Jones (captain), L. Attwood, P. Holder, J. Jones (referee), W.D. Sharratt. Kneeling: H. Deackes, J. Eustace.

Leckhampton. The Leckhampton Association football team that played in the Cheltenham League, senior division, in January 1940. Standing, left to right: P. Low, A. Read, E. Davis, B. Jenkins, J. Hunt, L.R. Bull (referee), W. Read, F. Marsh, S. Birt, P. Scottorn (chairman). Seated: H. Bowd, H. Clifton, G. Parry, L. Goddard.

Cheltenham. The VP Airscrews football team that played St Paul's Church Lads' Brigade on the Clyde recreation ground in November 1941. Standing, left to right: S.R. Terry (secretary and manager), J. Williams, L. Dean, M. Hughes, A. Dean, G. Hawker, C. Iddles, T. Pardoe. Front row: D. Powell, S. Tyler, D. Fox.

Cheltenham. The Sunningend football team of season 1943–44 that went unbeaten, winning both the Cheltenham War League and the North Gloucestershire Cup. The goalkeeper in the back row is A. Gregory; to the right of him is V. Boote. In the front row, second from the left with a clenched fist is R. Gill, and the captain H. Jones kneels with the cup and the football.

Winchcombe. A German prisoner-of-war football team made up of prisoners camped on the grounds of Sudeley Castle. The team used to play local teams at the Winchcombe Recreation Ground.

THE HOME
SERVICES

Stanway. In October 1941, members of the local Air Raid Precautions carried out a demonstration at Stanway House. These members are set to deal with the effects of an incendiary bomb.

Stanway. Casualties of a mock gas attack are being looked after by the ARP. This particular section of the ARP was made up of students of the ladies' secretarial college, at that time housed at Stanway House.

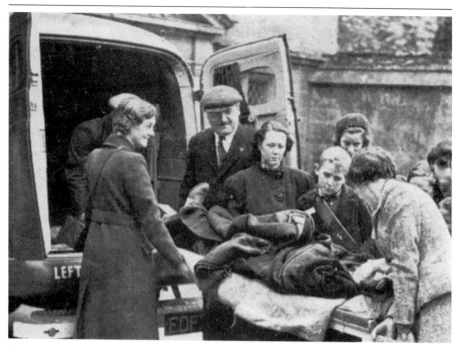

Stanway. 'Casualties' are stretchered into a van converted into an ambulance. The woman on the left was one of the demonstration officials, Miss N.M. Harris.

Stanway. Two of the young secretarial students show their knowledge of artificial respiration during the ARP demonstration.

Tewkesbury. Members of the Women's Voluntary Service line up during an Armistice Sunday parade in the early 1940s.

Cheltenham. Members of the Highbury Women's Voluntary Service creating camouflage nets at Corinth House, Bath Road. This was the home of Mrs D.L. Lipson (at the centre) who was the organizer of the Cheltenham WVS.

Chipping Campden. Taken just before the outbreak of hostilities is this photograph of the Ladies' Sewing Group outside Harry Warmington's house (the famous silversmith), Westington Corner. These ladies worked together to make many items useful to the war effort when war broke out.

Tewkesbury. Women volunteers at the British Restaurant (the 'Hot Pot') on its opening day in May 1941. On the far right is Mrs A.M. Sharp who was in charge of the kitchen. The other ladies helped in the kitchen and acted as waitresses.

Tewkesbury. Four nurses from the hospital enjoying the War Weapons Week parade in the town in April 1941.

Tewkesbury. On a wartime Sunday afternoon at the Cross the local Salvation Army conduct a hymn service. The woman wearing a beret facing the camera is Edna Smith.

Cheltenham. The ARP wardens of St Mark's, Cheltenham in 1941. Standing, left to right: I. Barnes, T. Whitehead, S. Morris, J. Harrison, C. Sturgess, F. Ormond, P. Allsworth, W. Wakefield, H. Morley, F. Moss, W. Wiltshire, D. O'Donoghue. Seated: Miss Gabriel, Miss White, Mr Holtham, A. Evans (second warden), H. Lott (senior warden), V.R. Evans, Mrs H. Lott, Mrs Hackleton.

Tewkesbury. Some of Tewkesbury's wartime special constables photographed during an Armistice Sunday parade, which accounts for the proud displaying of medals won in the First World War.

Winchcombe. Members of the Winchcombe Special Constabulary in 1941. Back row, left to right: D.F. Green, T.F. Alder, W. Fardon, T.M. Henney, A.G. Stevens, F. Clapton. Standing: W.H. Harding, A.E. Lanchbury, W.F. Cook, H.J. Archer, H. Major, F.W. Groves, J.L. Groom, W. Monks, W. Townsend, J.T. Rand, G.S. Quant, A.W. Neal, A.E. Roberts. Seated: W. Ballinger, Sergeant C. Francis (in charge), F.W. Adlard, A. Leslie-Smith, T. Lock, G.R. Pardington, R. Pearce.

Cheltenham. Members of E.1 Division Special Constabulary, Cheltenham Central North Section. Back row, left to right: W.A. Davis, J. Arnold, C. Minett, R. Archer, L.J. Lowe, W.J. Monkley, P.C. Clifford, T.J. Colson, H. Hall, G.R. Colwell. Middle row: C.J. Lovesey, H.E. Broad, C.D. Thomas, C.V. Smith, A.J. Flint, J.C. Venn, W.J. Gale, A.H. Meadows, G.A. Evans, G.W. Welch, J.A. Sallis, G.L. Lynton, P.J. Millichap. Seated: S.J. Davis, C.G. Irving, E.V. Cooke, T.L. Thompson, E.B. Evans, A.W. Hopkins, H.B. Poulton, H.J. Alden, A.R. Bloodworth, P.T. Rawlins, K. Rushworth.

Cheltenham. A mobile police officer preparing to climb into his patrol car, fully kitted out with his gas mask during a gas mask practice drill in February 1941.

Cheltenham. In a public display to encourage people to carry their gas masks, the members of Cheltenham's police force wore their gas masks in March 1941.

Cheltenham. During this gas mask practice, senior and junior police officers in the central station office were required to work in their masks for twenty minutes.

Tewkesbury. Members of Dowty's Auxiliary Fire Service 'dealing with a blaze' at the Dowty factory site at Ashchurch in Tewkesbury.

Cheltenham. Members of the Cheltenham Fire Brigade and the Auxiliary Fire Service dealing with a real fire at Messrs C. Taylor and Sons in Church Street, March 1941.

Cheltenham. Members of the fire service discuss the blaze that struck during a lunch hour. Messrs Taylor and Sons was a joinery and wood-working factory.

Winchcombe. Members of the Winchcombe Fire Brigade with their new trailer pump in August 1941. The pump is towed by an adapted 30 h.p. car. The captain, on the left, is Mr Arthur Hall.

Winchcombe. Some of the Winchcombe Home Guard on a Remembrance Sunday parade, 9 November 1941. They were part of the Cheltenham (1st) Battalion which was given the privilege of wearing the Gloucestershire Regiment badge.

Prestbury. Members of the Prestbury Platoon of the Home Guard. Back row, left to right: A.R. Wiggin, F.R. Allen, J. Parker, J.F. Hughes, F.J. Hughes, S. Hobbs, P.E. Hamblin, G.H. Stephens, F.C. Parker, E. Smith. Second row: J. Locke, J.Y. Haddon, H.L. Smith, W. Facer, A.W. Parker, W.I. Davies, A.C. Cole, H.G. Roberts, A.G. Short. Third row: H.B. Lewis, L. Inglis, F.C. Bullock, M. Britton, W.S. Mackie, B.A. Cripps, R.H.W. Bridgeman, Watson, F.H. James. Front row: A.J. Chamberlayne, A.W. Ellery, P.M.G. Morris, mascot Tony Purslow, H.R. Ellery, A.H.R. Spencer, J.C. Biscoe.

Tewkesbury. Members of the Tewkesbury Platoon of the Home Guard. Tewkesbury, along with Bristol Tramways, Dowty, Smith's Factory at Bishop's Cleeve, Winchcombe and Cheltenham made up the First Battalion of the Gloucestershire Home Guard.

Cheltenham. Members of the Home Guard on Aggs Hill, near Cleeve Hill, during a training session, October 1941.

Cheltenham. A 1941 photograph of the 125th (Cheltenham) Squadron Air Training Corps. Chiefly a schoolboy outfit, many of these lads went on to serve our country overseas.

THE ARMED
SERVICES

Winchcombe. Some of the first men from Gloucestershire to be called on to serve the nation's cause were these members of the Territorial Army from Winchcombe, leaving the town en route to Lilleshall in Shropshire.

The Winchcombe Territorials engaged in marching and drill practice at their training ground at Lilleshall. Soon afterwards they were dispatched for further training to Salisbury Plain.

A group photograph of the Winchcombe Division of the Territorial Army at Lilleshall.

Cheltenham. Two Valentine tanks outside the town hall in October 1941 during the 'Speed the Tanks' campaign – a campaign to raise yet more money from the town's population towards the purchase of a tank.

Cheltenham. Mayor John Howell CBE, FRCS addressing the crowd, on top of one of the Valentine tanks. John Howell was mayor of Cheltenham from 1938 to 1941.

Aggs Hill. At a public display of some of the tanks used by the British Army, this Valentine tank shows its ability to deal with steep inclines on Aggs Hill, near Cleeve Hill.

Aggs Hill. During the same display, this 25 ton Matilda tank works its way out of a quarry. Members of the Cheltenham Home Guard can be seen around the ridge of the quarry enjoying the spectacle.

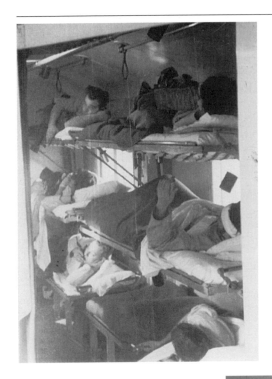

Cheltenham. Some of the many Americans who visited north Gloucestershire. These wounded servicemen have just arrived on board train at Leckhampton station, from where they were transported the relatively short distance to the 110th US Hospital at Ullenwood. (For the history of this hospital, see *South Gloucestershire at War*.)

Tewkesbury. A 1942 photograph of four Tewkesbury servicemen; clockwise from the top right: 'Nobby' O'Beirne, 'Oinky' Drinkwater, 'Buckle' Belcher and Rimbo Green. Rimbo Green joined the Navy on 14 February 1938, serving on three different ships during the war: HMS *Hasty* (1939–41), HMS *Castleton* (1942–43) and HMS *Bligh* (1943–45).

Cheltenham. A May wedding in 1941 at Leckhampton parish church of RAF serviceman Maurice H. Foran from Beckford to Barbara Baldwin of the Old Bath Road in Cheltenham. As more and more men were enlisted the number of last-minute weddings increased, especially as men were now expected to be overseas and away from home for a long time.

Staverton. The January 1941 wedding of Pilot Officer Clifford John Batho to Miss Beatrice May Crown at Staverton parish church. It was widely believed that at the time he was the shortest pilot serving in the RAF.

Twyning. The marriage of Rimbo Green to Hilda at Twyning church, 19 February 1942. Standing, left to right: Elsie Roberts, Audrey Green, Frank Sweet, Rimbo, Fred Green, Hilda, Jon Roberts, Joyce Roberts, Winnie Roberts.

Winchcombe. Sergeant Louis Tiffen RASC of Chelmsford, Essex, married Miss Muriel King of Hailes Street in Winchcombe at the parish church in December 1941.

Staverton. New Year's Day 1941, the wedding at the Staverton parish church between serviceman W.J. Evans, the son of Mr and Mrs H.G. Evans of Manor Cottage, Staverton, and Miss Helena M. Baker, eldest daughter of Mr and Mrs S. Baker of Littledean. Sir Gilbert and Lady McIlquham are standing behind the married couple to the left.

Cheltenham. Lance Corporal W. Goodwin RASC married Miss Betty Baggs, daughter of Mr and Mrs W.T. Baggs at St Luke's Church in February 1941. Mr Baggs was the owner of St Luke's Garage in St Luke's Road, a business that was established in 1913 and is still one of Cheltenham's most respected garages. It is run today by Mr H.G. Baggs, the son of Mr W.T. Baggs.

Charlton Kings. A serviceman's wedding at St Mary's church. Ernest Randell married Mary Hambling of Ryeworth Road in July 1941.

Tewkesbury serviceman Rimbo Green, tallest of the sailors, at the Acropolis in Athens which he visited with some friends while his ship HMS *Hasty* lay at anchor just off the coast on April Fools' Day 1941. The children are dressed in Greek national costume.

269 Squadron Air Sea Rescue was stationed in the Azores between 1945 and 1946. The squadron had several men from north Gloucestershire including Victor Kent, who worked as an electrician on the motor torpedo boats.

The landing craft used in bringing troops ashore in the Azores. Victor Kent travelled to the Azores on the SS *Miralda*, an oil tanker converted into an aircraft carrier. A highlight of this trip was that it was possible for the troops to play hockey on the flight deck.

Victor Kent of Shelley Road in Cheltenham enjoying a free moment in the Azores. He was able to send home pineapples, bananas and silk stockings to his young wife Audrey. All these items were in very short supply in Britain and were regarded as luxuries.

The members of Hut M8, the Azores. Back row, left to right: Alf Willmore, George Craven, Alf Westcott. Front row: Gordon Jolly, Jock Lamond, 'Jenks' Penman and Victor Kent.

One of the aircraft personnel carriers engaged to transport the troops back home from the Azores. Most of the servicemen returned to England on one of these aircraft; however, Vic Kent was one of the few who returned on board the Polish ship MS *Sobieski*.

Troops waiting to leave the Azores on board the MS *Sobieski*. To the troops, this ship was almost like a luxury liner. It had a famous history, participating in nearly all Allied landing operations of the war against Germany, including Norway, Dakar, Madagascar, North Africa, Sicily, Salerno, Anzio and southern France. During the invasion of Madagascar it carried on board the British General commanding a landing force.

Stanway. Gunner Albert G. Hughes of Stanway who served in the Royal Artillery. In August 1941 his parents Mr and Mrs J. Hughes received a postcard stating that he had been captured and was a prisoner of the German army.

Beckford. Sergeant Derek Woodward of the RAF, the elder son of Lieutenant A.G. Woodward RNVR of Beckford, who failed to return from a bombing trip over the Ruhr in June 1941. At the time he had been awaiting his commission after having been posted as an instructor in a training unit.

Cheltenham. Private R.J. Parker RASC of Witcombe Villa, Langdon Road, who was captured and became a prisoner of war in Crete in September 1941. Before the war he worked in a building society.

Cheltenham. Dr Robert Harvey was a major in the RAMC. On 28 April 1941 he was reported as missing but was later discovered to have been made a prisoner of war. He was noted for his bravery when, during the evacuation of Greece, he volunteered to stay behind with the wounded. He was the son-in-law of Mr and Mrs Fieldhouse of Shipton Oliffe manor.

Stalag VIII. Some of the British prisoners of war at Stalag VIII, B camp (*Stalag* was short for *Stammlager*, meaning base camp). In the photograph are several members of the Gloucestershire Regiment. Private Harry Walker of 24 Folly Lane, Cheltenham is marked with a cross.

Stalag VIII. More British prisoners of war at Stalag VIII. Private Kenneth Attwood of Station Road, Bishop's Cleeve is fourth from the right in the middle row. This particular camp was especially for non-commissioned officers and other ranks.

AROUND NORTH GLOUCESTERSHIRE

Bourton-on-the-Water. The opening of the new YMCA hut in August 1941 by Mrs Swainson, the wife of the YMCA divisional secretary. On the left is Dr R.B. Stewart. The hut was attached to the Bourton-on-the-Water United Services Club.

Tewkesbury. The interior of the British Restaurant, nicknamed the 'Hot Pot', opened by the mayor, R.A. Gaze, in May 1941. British Restaurants were part of the Government's idea to provide good food at a reasonable cost to the population and to provide a market for local farmers' produce. Awaiting the first meal to be prepared at the 'Hot Pot' are, from left to right, Revd H.G. Brown, A.M. Sharp, S.C.J. Moulder (the deputy mayor), Mrs Colchester Wemyss, R.A. Gaze, Miss L.M. Faithfull and Mrs Gaze (the mayoress).

Cheltenham. Mayor John Howell (on the left) opened a mobile YMCA exhibition in a specially constructed caravan in May 1941. The caravan was paid for by the Empire Tea-growers' Association and was placed in the Promenade outside the General Post Office. Councillor P.T. Smith, president of the Cheltenham YMCA, is at the microphone; Mr E.E. Wickens, who was in charge of the exhibition, is on the right.

Cheltenham. In November 1941 Mayor T.W. Waite opened the New Street Soup Kitchen, which was run by the Salvation Army. In this photograph, the mayor is accepting the first bowl of soup produced by the kitchen from Major J. Watherston of the Salvation Army.

Cheltenham. One of the town's finest dress shops was that of Ann Graham Ltd. In November 1941 they did a dual window display: the window on the left heralds Cheltenham's Warship Week, which ran from 22 to 29 November, and the window on the right has a preview of the 1942 season's dresses.

Leckhampton. The Crippetts after the snowstorm of early January 1941. Some of the windows of the house had not long been broken by the exploding of a delayed-action bomb.

Prestbury. The scene on the Prestbury Road in January 1942 when snowfall caused chaos throughout much of the county.

Cheltenham. The High Street and Colonnade, 1944. On the back of this postcard is a printed message by Winston Churchill typical of that found on many wartime printed cards: 'We have to gain the Victory. That is our task.'

Prestbury. Lower Noverton Farm, owned by Mr and Mrs Gilbert Adcock, seen here in 1941. Mr Adcock had served in the Gloucestershire Yeomanry during the First World War, seeing service in Gallipoli and at the Suez Canal. In one of the barns there was a good example of an English Gothic window made of stone.

Gotherington. Cotswold Cottage, the home during the war of Mrs Hayman and Ron and Dennis Baird, two Dagenham evacuees she took in in June 1940. Working at the cottage was a maid named Mary, a gardener, Mr Holmes, and Mrs Hayman also had her own chauffeur. The two houses next to the cottage were both struck by bombs on 19 November 1940 (see *Cheltenham at War*) and the cottage was extremely lucky to escape the same fate.

Brockhampton. The Manor opened its doors to the Upper First Division girls of Cheltenham Ladies' College in 1939. The pupils had been displaced from the college's premises in Cheltenham when they were requisitioned by the War Office.

Sevenhampton. The Manor, which entertained the domestic science classes from the Cheltenham Ladies' College, 1939.

Stanway. One of the summer fêtes that Stanway House was and still is famous for. This one took place in 1943.

Uckington. In January 1941 a fire destroyed this half-timbered barn and did much damage to the farmhouse, The Old Hall, adjoining it. It was the home of Mr and Mrs Thomas Brooks, but the cause of the fire was never discovered. The inset shows the fire damage to Mr and Mrs Brooks' house.

Tewkesbury. The Cross, devoid of street signs in wartime.

Tewkesbury. An early 1940s photograph of The Berkeley Arms. The brick building on the left was Boyce's ladies' clothes shop and the timber-framed building on the right was Tom Bassett's café/restaurant.

Tewkesbury. Barton Street, *c.* 1944. Notice the wartime headlamp covers on the parked cars. With black-out restrictions all vehicles had to have headlamp covers with tiny slits in them to allow a very small amount of light through. To partly compensate drivers and pedestrians, wheel arches and sills were often painted white and there were white stripes painted on to the edges of the pavement.

Tewkesbury. King John's Bridge, photographed from the site that is now the King John's Tavern. The morale-boosting message on the back of this card states: '"We shall continue steadfast in faith and duty till our task is done." *The Prime Minister.*'

Moreton-in-Marsh. A contemporary picture by artist Ken Aitken, commissioned by Mr G.V. Tyack, of the US Super Sixth Armoured Brigade in the High Street, May 1944. Like much of Gloucestershire, in the days leading up to D-Day, 6 June 1944, Moreton-in-Marsh was swarming with American servicemen, and the town was packed with Sherman tanks. The British School House in Moreton (now home to the Wellington Aviation Museum) was used by the Super Sixth Armoured Brigade as a stores and workshop – the brigade was under the leadership of Major-General Robert W. Grow. Moreton was also home throughout the war to the Wellington Bombers of the RAF 21 Operational Training Unit. (Picture courtesy of G.V. Tyack, Wellington Aviation Museum, Moreton-in-Marsh.)

SPECIAL EVENTS

Winchcombe. Members of the Home Guard and local nurses waiting for the arrival of the Queen Mother, Queen Mary, on one of her visits to Winchcombe. Holding the flag is Alf Willett; standing to the right of him is Sharman Mason. Living at Badminton during the war, Queen Mary made many visits to all parts of the county in her effort to raise morale.

Tewkesbury. The then Princess Royal on her visit to the Abbey, May 1941. Standing with her, left to right, are: Miss Gough, Canon E.P. Gough, Revd R.W. Taylor, Mrs E.P. Gough, the Princess, and Mayoress and Mayor Gaze.

Tewkesbury. The Princess Royal leaving Tewkesbury Abbey with the vicar. Walking behind her is the Chief Constable of Gloucestershire, Colonel W.F. Henn and Mrs Gough.

Tewkesbury. During the Princess Royal's visit to Tewkesbury Abbey she also made an inspection of the local Brownies and Girl Guides who welcomed her into the town. Here she gives the once–over to some local Brownies.

Cheltenham. On Thursday 4 December 1941 the world famous classical pianist Benno Moiseiwitsch gave two recitals in Cheltenham Town Hall. Born in Odessa in 1890, he became a naturalized Briton in 1937 and was respected throughout the music world.

Cheltenham. The Mayor of Cheltenham, Councillor T.W. Waite, announcing the final figures for the Wings for Victory Week in 1942, standing in front of the municipal offices. Towns throughout Britain had these fund-raising weeks to help the war effort: when enough money had been raised they would effectively 'adopt' an aircraft, tank, submarine or maybe a warship. This served to raise money and to keep morale high among the population.

Tewkesbury. Crowds gathering at the town hall to watch the War Weapons Week parade, which would mark the end of a hard fund-raising week. The sign above the door indicates that for the week the town had raised £66,913. The aim had been to raise about £40,000, which would pay for two bombers.

Tewkesbury. Crowds lining the street in April 1941 to watch the War Weapons Week parade. This parade included the file past of local Scouts, Guides and Brownies, the Home Guard and various pieces of wartime machinery.

Tewkesbury. The band of the Gloucestershire Regiment about to set off for their part in the parade.

Tewkesbury. Processions were very much a part of the town's life during the war, as they were for many others in Gloucestershire. This one took place during a National Service Week, probably in 1943 or 1944.

Tewkesbury. The procession to the Cross by the townsfolk during a wartime Armistice Sunday.

Tewkesbury. The British Legion parade followed by members of the local WVS, part of the Armistice Sunday parade.

Tewkesbury. Following the laying of wreaths at the Cross, prominent members of the local British Legion stand back in respect. Fourth from the left with his head bowed is Mr Warner; to the right of him is Jack Hughes; furthest right is Fred Green.

Tewkesbury. Several of Tewkesbury's councillors and leading members of the community during an Armistice Sunday gathering. Standing furthest right is Fred Green; third from the right wearing the medals is Jack Miller; two to the left of him is Cecil Crouch; and two to the left of him is Mayor Reginald Gaze.

Cheltenham. The meeting on Saturday 1 November 1941 of the secretaries of the Cheltenham Rural Area Savings Groups and officials at the local RDC offices. The meeting was called to discuss arrangements for raising £170,000 (the district quota) in the Cheltenham and District Warship Week, which was to begin on 22 November. In the front, on the right, is Captain H.P. Leschallas, chairman of the committee, and on the left is Major W. Shakespeare, the president.

Cheltenham. Electrical engineer W.J. Bache presenting a clock to John Pates on his retirement after 47 years in the Cheltenham Electrical Department, April 1941. Mr Pates laid power cables in all but one of Cheltenham's streets.

Cheltenham. Mr A.E. Case, circuit manager of the Gaumont British Corporation, presenting a Westminster chiming clock to Mr E.A. Gislingham (wearing glasses) on behalf of the cinema and café staff at the Gaumont Palace Cinema. Mr Gislingham, who had been manager of the cinema for five years, was leaving to join the RAF.

Dowdeswell. In June 1941 Mrs H.M. Clutterbuck opened up her home, Dowdeswell Manor, for a public fête. Among the many attractions, stalls and games was this swing band that played throughout the afternoon.

Dowdeswell. 'Gypsy' palm-reading was another attraction at the summer fête, which was in aid of the Dowdeswell and Andoversford District Nursing Association.

Dowdeswell. One of the bring-and-buy stalls at Dowdeswell Manor during its summer fête.

Dowdeswell. There were many games at the fête, as there were at most village fêtes. Bottle-ringing was clearly one of the favourites.

Tewkesbury. On 3 December 1940 at the Homes Market (the local cattle market), an auction was held in aid of the Red Cross Relief Fund. The subject of the auction was this patriotically covered donkey donated by Mr Bob Perry. Standing on the bales of hay, on the left at the back, is the auctioneer Leonard Hone. In the front, from left to right, are Fred Green, Bob Perry, Sam Loveridge and Tom Woodward.

Charlton Kings, 8 May 1945, VE Day. A party held at Croft Gardens was similar to thousands of parties being held all over the country.

Tewkesbury. Some of the women of Prior's Park who, in spite of rationing and financial restrictions, managed to serve up a delicious treat for their friends and children during the street parties that were held on 8 May 1945.

Tewkesbury. Margaret Road in Prior's Park; the children are enjoying the first hours of peacetime. In the picture, among their friends, are Rosemary and Cynthia Collins, Fred and Betty Everess, Doris and Rose Gibbs, Hazel Lewis, Vera and Blanch Hawlings, Phyllis Lippett, Alice Walker, Lil Ryder, Margaret Jackson, Mary Pitt, Nancy Jackson, Rita Upton, Bill and Clara Cash.

Tewkesbury. The VE Day street party in York Road, Prior's Park. In this photograph are Margaret Harris, Cathy Cull, Norma Hammant, Bill Cash, Hilda Danter, Gladys Gibbs, Ruth Beale, Colin and Clifford Bolton, Wyn Harris, Joan Gibbs, Mrs Hooper, Clara Fletcher, Mrs Good, Hilda Phipps, Tina Scasebrook, Mr and Mrs Matty and Bill and Jesse Bassett.

Acknowledgements

It is with sincere appreciation that I would like to thank the following people, without whose contributions, advice and knowledge this book would not have been possible:

Mr D. Baird • Mr G. Baker • Mr N.A. Barnes • Cheltenham Ladies' College
Mrs B. Coster • Mr M. Cuttell • Dean Close School • Dowty Aerospace
Ms V. Francis • Mrs B.A. Gill • Mr Rimbo Green • Mrs P. Hitchman
Mr and Mrs V. Kent • The late Mrs M. Lewis • C.F. Martin Collection
Mr G. Overton • Photo Studio of Tewkesbury • Mr N. Preece • Mrs B. Smith
Mrs E. Thomas • Mr J. Townsend • Miss J. Tucker • Mr G. Tyack
Mr L. Willett.

And for her love and support, my wife Jayne. For her energy, and enthusiasm for all that I do, a special thank you to my mother.

To those that I haven't named, my apologies, but still my thanks.

Please note that every effort has been made to contact and establish copyright holders of all photographs.

To order any of these titles please telephone Littlehampton Book Services on 01903 721596

ALDERNEY

Alderney: A Second Selection, *B Bonnard*

BEDFORDSHIRE

Bedfordshire at Work, *N Lutt*

BERKSHIRE

Maidenhead, *M Hayles & D Hedges*
Around Maidenhead, *M Hayles & B Hedges*
Reading, *P Southerton*
Reading: A Second Selection, *P Southerton*
Sandhurst and Crowthorne, *K Dancy*
Around Slough, *J Hunter & K Hunter*
Around Thatcham, *P Allen*
Around Windsor, *B Hedges*

BUCKINGHAMSHIRE

Buckingham and District, *R Cook*
High Wycombe, *R Goodearl*
Around Stony Stratford, *A Lambert*

CHESHIRE

Cheshire Railways, *M Hitches*
Chester, *S Nichols*

CLWYD

Clwyd Railways, *M Hitches*

CLYDESDALE

Clydesdale, *Lesmahagow Parish Historical Association*

CORNWALL

Cornish Coast, *T Bowden*
Falmouth, *P Gilson*
Lower Fal, *P Gilson*
Around Padstow, *M McCarthy*
Around Penzance, *J Holmes*
Penzance and Newlyn, *J Holmes*
Around Truro, *A Lyne*
Upper Fal, *P Gilson*

CUMBERLAND

Cockermouth and District, *J Bernard Bradbury*
Keswick and the Central Lakes, *J Marsh*
Around Penrith, *F Boyd*
Around Whitehaven, *H Fancy*

DERBYSHIRE

Derby, *D Buxton*
Around Matlock, *D Barton*

DEVON

Colyton and Seaton, *T Gosling*
Dawlish and Teignmouth, *G Gosling*
Devon Aerodromes, *K Saunders*
Exeter, *P Thomas*
Exmouth and Budleigh Salterton, *T Gosling*
From Haldon to Mid-Dartmoor, *T Hall*
Honiton and the Otter Valley, *J Yallop*
Around Kingsbridge, *K Tanner*
Around Seaton and Sidmouth, *T Gosling*
Seaton, Axminster and Lyme Regis, *T Gosling*

DORSET

Around Blandford Forum, *B Cox*
Bournemouth, *M Colman*
Bridport and the Bride Valley, *J Burrell & S Humphries*
Dorchester, *T Gosling*
Around Gillingham, *P Crocker*

DURHAM

Darlington, *G Flynn*
Darlington: A Second Selection, *G Flynn*
Durham People, *M Richardson*
Houghton-le-Spring and Hetton-le-Hole, *K Richardson*
Houghton-le-Spring and Hetton-le-Hole:
    A Second Selection, *K Richardson*
Sunderland, *S Miller & B Bell*
Teesdale, *D Coggins*
Teesdale: A Second Selection, *P Raine*
Weardale, *J Crosby*
Weardale: A Second Selection, *J Crosby*

DYFED

Aberystwyth and North Ceredigion,
    Dyfed Cultural Services Dept
Haverfordwest, *Dyfed Cultural Services Dept*
Upper Tywi Valley, *Dyfed Cultural Services Dept*

ESSEX

Around Grays, *B Evans*

GLOUCESTERSHIRE

Along the Avon from Stratford to Tewkesbury, *J Jeremiah*
Cheltenham: A Second Selection, *R Whiting*
Cheltenham at War, *P Gill*
Cirencester, *J Welsford*
Around Cirencester, *E Cuss & P Griffiths*
Forest, The, *D Mullin*
Gloucester, *J Voyce*
Around Gloucester, *A Sutton*
Gloucester: From the Walwin Collection, *J Voyce*
North Cotswolds, *D Viner*
Severn Vale, *A Sutton*
Stonehouse to Painswick, *A Sutton*
Stroud and the Five Valleys, *S Gardiner & L Padin*
Stroud and the Five Valleys: A Second Selection,
    S Gardiner & L Padin
Stroud's Golden Valley, *S Gardiner & L Padin*
Stroudwater and Thames & Severn Canals,
    E Cuss & S Gardiner
Stroudwater and Thames & Severn Canals: A Second
    Selection, *E Cuss & S Gardiner*
Tewkesbury and the Vale of Gloucester, *C Hilton*
Thornbury to Berkeley, *J Hudson*
Uley, Dursley and Cam, *A Sutton*
Wotton-under-Edge to Chipping Sodbury, *A Sutton*

GWYNEDD

Anglesey, *M Hitches*
Gwynedd Railways, *M Hitches*
Around Llandudno, *M Hitches*
Vale of Conwy, *M Hitches*

HAMPSHIRE

Gosport, *J Sadden*
Portsmouth, *P Rogers & D Francis*

HEREFORDSHIRE

Herefordshire, *A Sandford*

HERTFORDSHIRE

Barnet, *I Norrie*
Hitchin, *A Fleck*
St Albans, *S Mullins*
Stevenage, *M Appleton*

ISLE OF MAN

The Tourist Trophy, *B Snelling*

ISLE OF WIGHT

Newport, *D Parr*
Around Ryde, *D Parr*

JERSEY

Jersey: A Third Selection, *R Lemprière*

KENT

Bexley, *M Scott*
Broadstairs and St Peter's, *J Whyman*
Bromley, Keston and Hayes, *M Scott*
Canterbury: A Second Selection, *D Butler*
Chatham and Gillingham, *P MacDougall*
Chatham Dockyard, *P MacDougall*
Deal, *J Broady*
Early Broadstairs and St Peter's, *B Wootton*
East Kent at War, *D Collyer*
Eltham, *J Kennett*
Folkestone: A Second Selection, *A Taylor & E Rooney*
Goudhurst to Tenterden, *A Guilmant*
Gravesend, *R Hiscock*
Around Gravesham, *R Hiscock & D Grierson*
Herne Bay, *J Hawkins*
Lympne Airport, *D Collyer*
Maidstone, *I Hales*
Margate, *R Clements*
RAF Hawkinge, *R Humphreys*
RAF Manston, *RAF Manston History Club*
RAF Manston: A Second Selection,
    RAF Manston History Club
Ramsgate and Thanet Life, *D Perkins*
Romney Marsh, *E Carpenter*
Sandwich, *C Wanostrocht*
Around Tonbridge, *C Bell*
Tunbridge Wells, *M Rowlands & I Beavis*
Tunbridge Wells: A Second Selection,
    M Rowlands & I Beavis
Around Whitstable, *C Court*
Wingham, Adisham and Littlebourne, *M Crane*

LANCASHIRE

Around Barrow-in-Furness, *J Garbutt & J Marsh*
Blackpool, *C Rothwell*
Bury, *J Hudson*
Chorley and District, *J Smith*
Fleetwood, *C Rothwell*
Heywood, *J Hudson*
Around Kirkham, *C Rothwell*
Lancashire North of the Sands, *J Garbutt & J Marsh*
Around Lancaster, *S Ashworth*
Lytham St Anne's, *C Rothwell*
North Fylde, *C Rothwell*
Radcliffe, *J Hudson*
Rossendale, *B Moore & N Dunnachie*

LEICESTERSHIRE

Around Ashby-de-la-Zouch, *K Hillier*
Charnwood Forest, *I Keil, W Humphrey & D Wix*
Leicester, *D Burton*
Leicester: A Second Selection, *D Burton*
Melton Mowbray, *T Hickman*
Around Melton Mowbray, *T Hickman*
River Soar, *D Wix, P Shacklock & I Keil*
Rutland, *T Clough*
Vale of Belvoir, *T Hickman*
Around the Welland Valley, *S Mastoris*

LINCOLNSHIRE

Grimsby, *J Tierney*
Around Grimsby, *J Tierney*
Grimsby Docks, *J Tierney*
Lincoln, *D Cuppleditch*